We'd like to extend a special thanks to the teachers of Hebron Ministerial Institute for their valuable teachings, many of which were used as a foundation for this book.

We'd also like to thank the following editors for their many hours of hard work to make this book a greater blessing:

Pastor Juan Domingo Alurralde, Sindy Quiñonez, Rebecca Bustamante, Josefina Machado, Ana Machado, and Joy Mutepfa.

Unless otherwise noted, all Scripture quotations are taken from the King James Version of the Holy Bible. Note: Scripture quotations that are not followed by a reference have been paraphrased for young readers.

Written and designed by: Nora Marroquín
Illustrated by: Adriana Marroquín
Contributing artist: Yorik Illescas

Copyright © 2015 Hebron Ministries
All rights reserved.

No part of this book may be reproduced in any manner without the written consent of the publisher except for brief excerpts in critical reviews or articles.

ISBN 13: 978-1-61244-387-4
Library of Congress Control Number: 2015944940

Printed in the United States of America

Published by Halo Publishing International
1100 NW Loop 410
Suite 700 - 176
San Antonio, Texas 78213
Toll Free 1-877-705-9647
www.halopublishing.com
www.holapublishing.com
e-mail: contact@halopublishing.com

# Bible Stories and Lessons

**Book Five**

Joseph

### HEBRON MINISTRIES
"...Christ in you, the hope of glory." Colossians 1:27

# Preface

The nine-book series of *Bible Stories and Lessons* will help children understand God's plan and purpose for their lives. Our prayer is that as this plan is unfolded time and time again throughout each book, every heart may be awakened and encouraged to wholeheartedly run after God for the rest of its life. May God's children become *"...arrows in the hand of a mighty man..."* so that they may hit the divine mark that God has intended for their lives.

We are excited to be able to share this wonderful series with you. It is a miracle and an answer to prayer! May God use it to bless your family and church in a special way.

# CONTENTS

## Joseph ... 7

| | |
|---|---|
| The Dreamer | 9 |
| Joseph Is Sold | 13 |
| Joseph in Potiphar's House | 15 |
| Joseph in Jail | 19 |
| Joseph Lifted Up | 23 |
| Years of Plenty and Years of Want | 32 |
| Back in Canaan | 34 |
| Jacob's Sons Visit Egypt | 35 |
| The Famine Worsens | 40 |
| Joseph and Benjamin Meet Again | 42 |
| Joseph's Silver Cup | 47 |
| Jacob and Joseph Together Again | 52 |
| Jacob Dies | 56 |
| Joseph's Last Days | 57 |

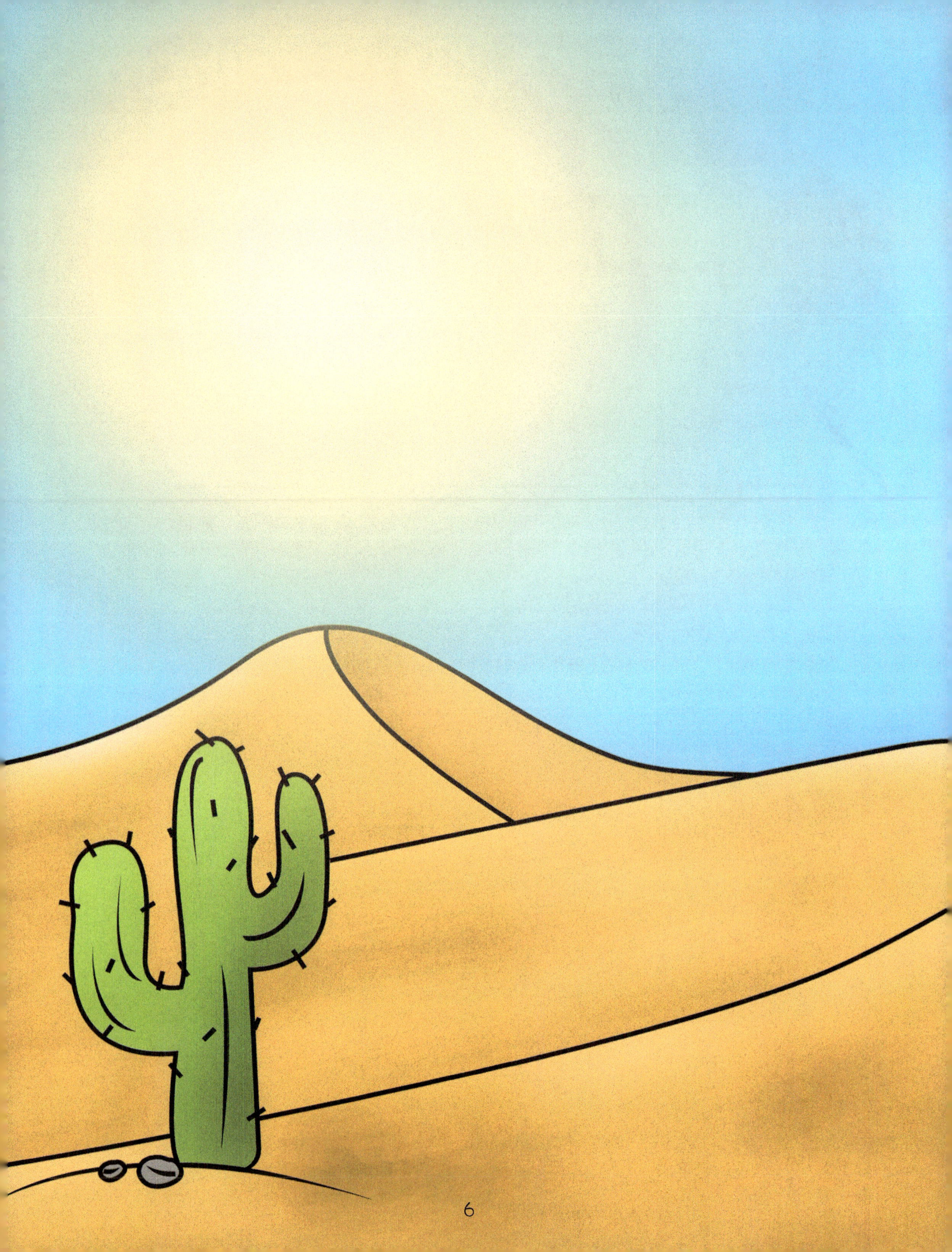

# Joseph
(Genesis 37-50)

Jacob lived in the land of Canaan with **ALL** of his sons.

The sons he had with Leah were Reuben, Simeon, Levi, Judah, Issachar, and Zebulon.

His sons with Zilpah were Gad and Asher.

His sons with Bilhah were Dan and Naphtali.

And the sons he had with Rachel were Joseph and Benjamin.

They were twelve in all.

7

Without a doubt, Joseph was Jacob's favorite child. Jacob loved Joseph more because he was the son of his old age and the firstborn of his beloved wife Rachel. But Jacob's special love for Joseph became a problem because the other brothers knew that their father did not love them as much.

Jacob gave Joseph a coat of many colors to show that, in his eyes, Joseph was the most important of the twelve sons.

Joseph's brothers also knew that Jacob had chosen Joseph to receive a double portion of his inheritance when he died. That made them jealous. They hated Joseph for it.

Joseph and his brothers would go out to feed the flocks, and whenever his brothers misbehaved, Joseph would give Jacob the report of their evil behavior. That made his brothers hate him even more.

It seemed as though everything Joseph said and did irritated them and made them more and more angry.

## The Dreamer

One night, Joseph had a strange dream that made him wonder about its meaning. He decided to tell his brothers about it.

"Hey guys," he said to them, "listen to the dream I had last night. I dreamt that all of us were working in the fields, binding our bundles of grain, when suddenly my bundle stood up straight and tall and your bundles stood around it. Then, all of your bundles bowed down to mine!"

Mocking him, his brothers responded, "So ... what is the dream supposed to mean? That you'll be the king over us some day?"

Joseph's dream only made his brothers resentful, and they hated him even more.

Then Joseph had another dream. He dreamed that the sun, the moon, and eleven stars bowed down to him.

Once again, he told the dream to his father and to his brothers, but Jacob scolded him for it. He said, "Joseph! What kind of dreams are these that you're having? Do you really believe that someday your family will bow down to you?"

Maybe Joseph even felt a little ashamed after his father's rebuke. He certainly didn't want to upset his father. Jacob never said anything to his sons about it, but Joseph's dreams really made him wonder.

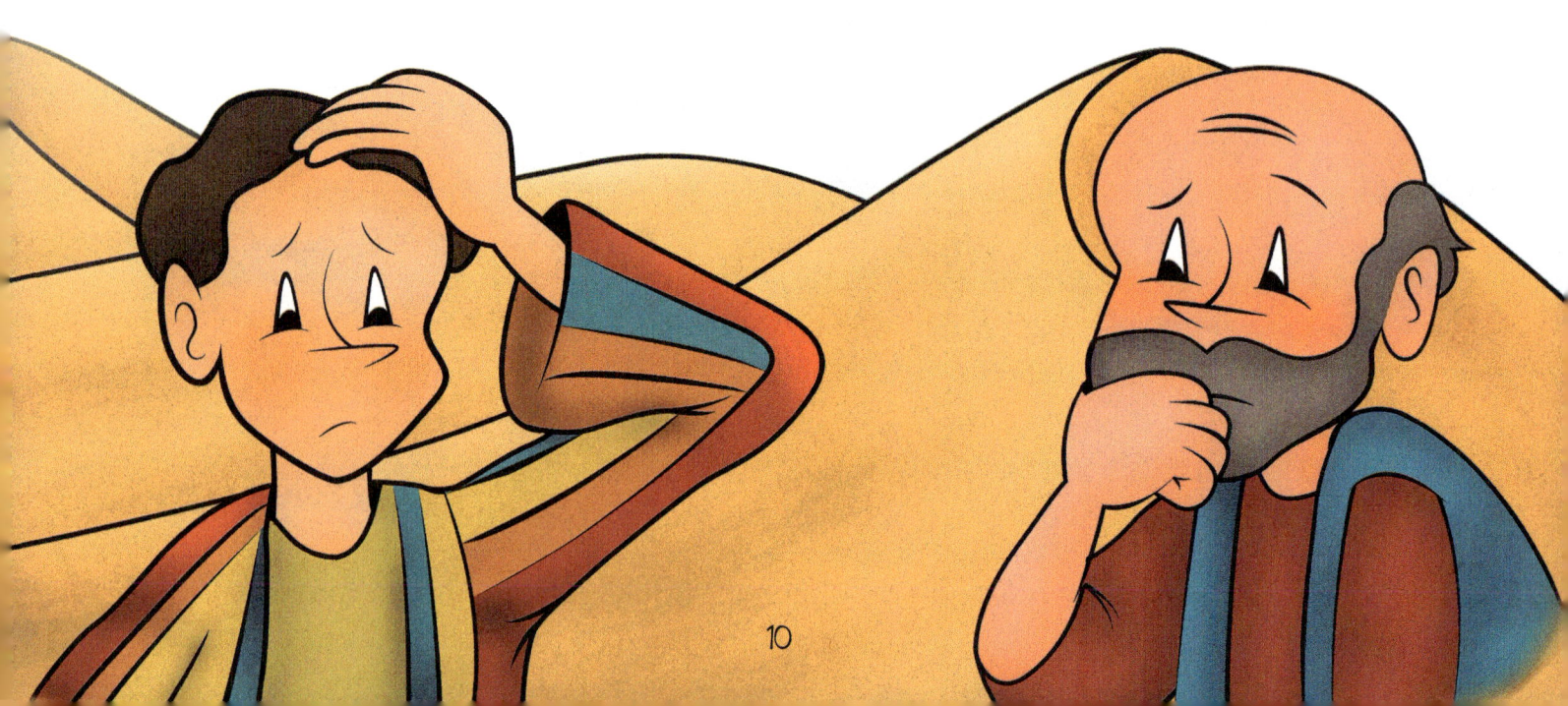

# What Lessons Does GOD Have for Us?

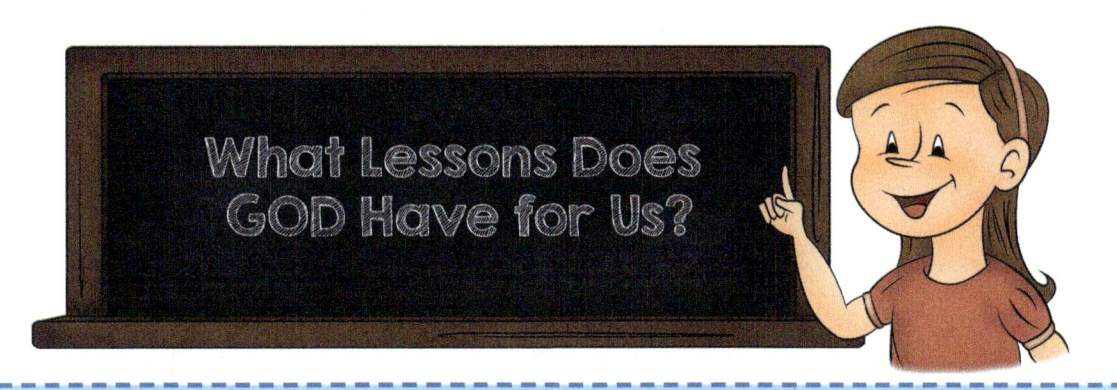

## LESSON: THE COAT OF MANY COLORS

Jacob gave Joseph a coat of many colors because Joseph was his favorite son. In Jacob's eyes, Joseph was truly his firstborn because Joseph was the first son born of his beloved wife Rachel. Jacob's other sons were jealous and envied Joseph because they understood that the coat of many colors represented two things:

1. It showed that <u>Jacob considered Joseph to be his true firstborn</u>. This meant that Joseph would receive a double portion of Jacob's inheritance when he died.

2. In the Bible, the firstborn son would take his father's place once the father died. That means that <u>the firstborn received natural and spiritual leadership over the entire family</u>. Joseph's coat reminded his brothers that he would someday be greater than they and rule over them.

## LESSON: JOSEPH WAS LOYAL

When Joseph noticed that his brothers were misbehaving, he didn't keep quiet about it. Instead, Joseph told his father about the things they did wrong. Do you think Joseph was gossiping by doing so?

No. Joseph was being loyal to his God-given authority—in this case, his father. Of course, Joseph had to have known that his brothers would hate him even more for doing it. He also knew, however, that it was his **RESPONSIBILITY** to do it. If Joseph really wanted to do what was right, he had no choice but to go and tell his father.

God wants us to have the same loyal heart that Joseph had. If we see or find out about someone that has done something sinful or wrong, it is our responsibility to let our God given authority (parents or pastor) know about it.

## LESSON: IS IT ALRIGHT TO HATE MY BROTHER?

Remember that our brother is anyone who truly does the will of God (Matthew 12:50). That is, anyone who is not only a believer in Jesus Christ, but who also obeys God's commandments is called our brother or sister in the Lord.

Do you think it is okay to hate our brother or sister in the Lord? What does God say about it?

*"Whosoever hateth his brother is a murderer: and ye know that no murderer hath eternal life abiding in him."* (I John 3:15)

If God will go as far as to call us murderers for hating our brother or sister, then we know it is a SERIOUS thing in His eyes. May the Lord give us a clean heart and fill it with HIS precious love for our brothers and sisters in Him.

## Joseph Is Sold

One day Joseph's brothers went out to feed the flocks in Shechem. Jacob wanted to make sure his sons were doing alright, so he sent Joseph out to check on them. As soon as his brothers saw Joseph coming, they got angry and started thinking of a way to kill him.

"Oh brother! Here comes the big dreamer," they said to each other. "Why don't we just kill him and throw him in that well over there? We can just tell father that some wild animal ate him up. Then, we'll see what becomes of his great dreams. Ha! Ha! Ha!"

Reuben overheard his brothers' evil plan. He didn't want to harm Joseph. He wanted Joseph to return to Jacob, his father, alive and well. So he quickly spoke up for his brother saying, "We can throw him in the well if you want to, but don't kill him."

The brothers waited until Joseph approached them. Then, they grabbed him and ripped off his coat!

"Hey! What's going on? What are you doing? That's my coat!" Joseph must have said. "You just be quiet, dreamer boy, and ... wait here!" they said as they threw him into the empty well.

Poor Joseph! He must have screamed and screamed for help. But no one responded. His brothers just sat down to eat, and not one of them rose up to help him.

As Joseph's brothers were eating, a group of Ishmaelite merchant men passed by. They were taking spices to sell in Egypt. When Judah saw them, he said to his brothers,

"You know what? Joseph is our brother. Let's not kill him. After all, what good would it do us? Why don't we just sell him to those merchant men instead?"

Moved with envy, the brothers started thinking that Judah's idea was a very good one. If they sold Joseph, they wouldn't have to shed blood, and they would still get to keep their father's riches. So they sold their brother to the Ishmaelite men for twenty shekels of silver.

Reuben was the only brother who was not there when the brothers sold Joseph. When he returned to the well and saw that Joseph wasn't there anymore, he was devastated. How would he ever explain this to his father?

**He just couldn't.** Instead, he and his brothers covered up the truth. They took Joseph's coat of many colors, put goat's blood on it, and took it to Jacob. This made Jacob believe that a wild animal had killed Joseph. Jacob was heartbroken. His sons and daughters tried cheering him up, but nothing helped. He cried for Joseph many, many days.

## Joseph in Potiphar's House

Joseph was taken to Egypt—far away from his family. It was a very different country with a very different language and customs from the ones Joseph had grown up with. How could his brothers have done this to him? Joseph was heartbroken. Surely he felt that God had forgotten him; surely he felt that he was ALL alone.

### But he was not.

The Lord was with Joseph, even though it didn't seem like it at the moment. God was fulfilling His perfect plan, and Joseph was soon to see that God had never and would never leave him.

Upon arrival in Egypt, Joseph was sold as a slave to a very important Egyptian man. His name was Potiphar. He was a captain of Pharaoh's army.

Little by little, Joseph found grace and favor with his master. It wasn't long before Potiphar noticed that there was something very special about this young man. Since the Lord was with Joseph, every job that Joseph did was a job **WELL DONE.** The blessing of the Lord was truly upon him. Potiphar began to give Joseph more and more responsibilities, and soon Potiphar made him the ruler over his entire household.

Joseph worked faithfully for Potiphar, because he knew that God was watching him. He was a young man that feared God and wanted to please God no matter what.

Potiphar couldn't have been a happier man, for the Lord blessed his house because of Joseph.

Things went well for Joseph during that time, but God was still at work in his life. In order for God's plan to be complete, Joseph had several trials still ahead of him.

One day Potiphar's wife asked Joseph to do something that was wrong. Joseph loved God and didn't want to displease Him. Surely he also appreciated the confidence that his master Potiphar had placed in him, and he didn't want to disappoint him either. Wisely, Joseph ran before he could even think twice about disobeying God or disappointing Potiphar. But Potiphar's wife was evil, and since Joseph didn't do what she asked him to, she got upset. She went to Potiphar and lied, telling him that Joseph had tried to hurt her.

When Potiphar heard what his wife said, he got angry and put Joseph in jail. Mrs. Potiphar got what she wanted, but Potiphar lost a very valuable servant.

# What Lessons Does GOD Have for Us?

## LESSON: GOD WAS WITH JOSEPH

Joseph was suffering greatly. He didn't have any guarantee that one day things would be better. He was sad that he might never see his father again, but even though Joseph was very far away from his earthly father, his heavenly Father was very close by.

*"The righteous cry, and the Lord heareth, and delivereth them out of all their troubles. The Lord is nigh [close] unto them that are of a broken heart; and saveth such as be of a contrite spirit. Many are the afflictions of the righteous: but the Lord delivereth him out of them all."* (Psalm 34:17-19)

God doesn't promise that a righteous person will not suffer or have problems, BUT He DOES promise that HE will always be with us to help us and deliver us from our problems in due time.

## LESSON: JOSEPH RAN

Mrs. Potiphar tried to tempt Joseph to do wrong. To tempt means that she tried to get Joseph to WANT to do something bad. But Joseph was smart. Before he even had a chance to think about it, he ran!

That's exactly what God tells us to do when we are tempted to do something wrong. Read the following verse:

*"Flee [run] from temptation."* (II Timothy 2:22, paraphrased)

Do you still not understand? Here's a small example:

Let's say your mom makes your favorite cake for some guests that are coming over for dinner. You really want to eat a slice right now, but your mom says, "Don't you touch that cake! You can have a slice when our guests come over." It would be wrong if you ate a slice of the cake—your mom already told you not to. What would be the best thing for you to do?

Do you think it would be wise to sit in front of the cake all afternoon just staring at it? Of course not! The temptation would be too great for you to withstand. The best thing for you to do is to stay away from the kitchen so you will be as FAR away from the cake (your temptation) as possible.

If you feel tempted to do something that is not pleasing to the Lord or to your parents, don't give yourself the time to think about it. Just run! To run means to stay away from that temptation altogether and to keep it away from you at all times.

# Joseph in Jail

Prison was a dark and ugly place to be. Surely it was not a comfortable place either, but the LORD had sent Joseph there to try his heart. The Lord was also WITH Joseph the whole time he was in prison. It was part of the preparation that God had in His plans for Joseph, so that He could fulfill His purposes in and through him.

Once again, Joseph found favor with his authority. The prison keeper put Joseph in charge of the whole prison. Joseph worked hard for the prison keeper during his time there, and the Lord blessed everything that he did. The prison keeper was happy to have Joseph working for him, just like Potiphar had been. Joseph was truly a blessing, and as time passed, God even gave Joseph a very special gift—the ability to understand and interpret dreams!

One day, some new prisoners came to the prison. They were Pharaoh's chief butler (cupbearer) and his baker. They had offended Pharaoh and made him angry, so he had them arrested. The men were placed under Joseph's care while in prison. One night they both had a dream.

The following morning, when Joseph went to see them, he noticed that they looked worried. Joseph kindly asked them, "Why are you both so sad today? What is it that's bothering you so much?"

"We each had a dream last night," they said, "and ... there's no one who can tell us what the dreams mean."

Joseph looked at them and said, "Men! Don't you know that the ONE who gives interpretations is God? Tell me your dreams and God will give you an answer."

"Okay, I will speak first then," said the butler. "I dreamt that I was looking at a vineyard. In that vineyard there were three branches and the three of them budded and brought forth good grapes. I had Pharaoh's cup in my hand and I squeezed the grape juice into his cup. Then, I gave the cup to Pharaoh."

Joseph said, "The three branches are three days. The dream means that in three days Pharaoh will give you your job back and you will once again be his cupbearer just as you have always been. But please, please, please remember me when you leave here. Remember that I was kind to you, and mention my name to Pharaoh! Please! I want to get out of here."

When Pharaoh's baker saw that the butler's interpretation was good, he spoke up too. "Okay, now I will speak," he said. "In my dream I had three white baskets on my head. The top basket was full of all sorts of sweet breads for Pharaoh, but the birds came and ate them all up."

Joseph said to him, "Your three baskets also speak of three days, but the interpretation is that in three days, Pharaoh will lift up thy head from off thee, and will hang thee on a tree."

Sure enough, everything happened just as Joseph had said. Three days later, the butler was given his job back and the baker was put to death.

But the butler didn't even mention Joseph's name to Pharaoh.

# He completely forgot.

21

# What Lessons Does GOD Have for Us?

## ⭐ LESSON: JOSEPH TRUSTED IN HIS HEAVENLY FATHER

The word of God tried Joseph while he was in prison. What does that mean? Well, it's easy to believe and trust in God when it seems like God is doing great things for us, but what about when things don't seem to be going so well, as in Joseph's case? It's then that God tries us to see if we will continue to believe and trust in Him.

Remember what we learned in the seventh day of creation? Joseph was a man of faith who had learned to find rest and contentment in what God was doing and choosing for him. He believed and trusted in God and he NEVER lost hope.

Just as He did in Joseph's case, God will try our hearts as well. God wants us to find that same rest and contentment in Him—no matter how difficult things might become. God never forces us. He lets us choose whether or not we will allow Him to finish the creation work in our hearts. If we let Him finish molding us, like clay in the hands of a potter, we will receive many blessings in return and God will give us His very best. We will be **VERY** happy in the end.

## ⭐ LESSON: JOSEPH WAS DILIGENT

It didn't seem fair that Joseph had been sold as a slave to work for Potiphar, and it certainly didn't seem fair that he was placed in prison for something he didn't do.

In spite of this, Joseph became a servant to the masters that GOD had placed over him, and he WORKED HARD for them. No matter what they asked Joseph to do, he always did it JUST the way they asked him to.

Proverbs 22:29 says:

> "Seest thou a man diligent in his business? He shall stand before kings; he shall not stand before mean men."

# Joseph Lifted Up

Two whole years went by after what had happened with the butler and baker. Joseph was still in jail and he probably felt he would be there forever.

But God had not forgotten his beloved son Joseph. He just wanted to use those two years to prepare Joseph for what was coming. Joseph never stopped believing and trusting in God's mercies, and later he would see that God had worked everything out for his good.

**One night something happened.**

Pharaoh had a dream that really caught his attention. When he woke up, he was bothered by it because he knew the dream had to mean something. He called for his magicians and wise men to help him understand the dream, but everyone's mind was blank; no one was able to help.

This probably made Pharaoh even more anxious about his dream. What could it possibly mean? Where on earth would he find someone wise enough to interpret it for him? As he sat there thinking, suddenly his cupbearer spoke up.

"Oh, Pharaoh! Forgive me, but I just remembered something! You see, when you sent me to prison a couple of years ago, there was a young Hebrew man in charge of the prison. He had the power to understand and interpret dreams. In fact, the baker and I had a dream in the same night and he interpreted both of them. Everything happened JUST as he said it would."

"**Quick!**" said Pharaoh to his servant, "bring that man to me at once!"

Joseph had NO idea what was going on in the king's palace that day. For him, it was a day in prison like any other. BUT ... **it was NOT a day like any other** because it was the day that God had chosen to take Joseph out! And that's because God saw that Joseph had already completely surrendered his life to His mercy. In his heart, Joseph had given God a clear message: "Lord, I trust you in this, and I BELIEVE that one day, when you see fit, YOU will take me out of this dungeon. And it doesn't matter if you decide to never take me out. Things will still be fine between you and me."

Joseph was resting in the Lord. That is, he was no longer fighting to get taken out of jail. He was content in doing God's perfect will instead of his own will. This was a sign that the Lord's work had been completed in Joseph's life. God had allowed Joseph to stay in that ugly dungeon until His word had refined him. But now ... it was time for Joseph to be taken out.

Joseph was quickly taken out of prison. He showered, shaved, and was taken before the king. There he stood—waiting to hear what Pharaoh had to say to him. Joseph had grown to know the Lord in such a deep way that he probably wasn't even afraid. He knew that God was right by his side.

And **Pharaoh spoke to Joseph saying:** "I had a dream and I know it has to mean something, but no one is able to interpret it for me. I have heard that you have the power to understand and interpret dreams. Is that right?"

"It's not me," **said Joseph.** "God is the ONE who will give you the interpretation so you can be at peace."

"My dream was this," said Pharaoh,

"I was standing by the river when suddenly seven fat beautiful cows came out of the river. They walked to the meadow to eat, but as they were eating, seven of the skinniest, ugliest cows I have ever seen also came out of the river."

"Then, ... the seven skinny cows ate up the fat cows, and even though they had eaten them, they still looked just as ugly and skinny as before. Then ... I woke up. But I fell asleep again and had another dream. This time I saw seven full and healthy ears of grain on a stalk. Just behind them I could see seven very dry ears of grain. Then, the seven dry ears of grain swallowed up the seven healthy ears of grain. And then I woke up. I tell you though, I have sought out EVERY magician and wise man in town and NOT ONE could interpret my dream."

When Joseph opened his mouth to give Pharaoh an answer, he spoke firmly and with authority because God was speaking through him. He said to Pharaoh:

"Your two dreams are actually one, oh Pharaoh. They both mean the same thing. God is trying to show you what He is going to do very soon. The seven fat cows and the seven healthy ears of grain are the same thing. They represent seven years. And the seven skinny cows and seven dry ears of grain also represent seven years. God is showing you that soon there will be seven years of great plenty throughout all the land of Egypt, but those seven years will be followed by seven very terrible years of famine. That famine will be so great that no one will even remember the seven years of plenty."

Then Joseph told Pharaoh, "This is what you should do. Choose out a man who is wise and discreet who can help you rule over Egypt. That man should gather twenty percent of all the grain and food during the seven years of abundance and save it for the years of famine. That way no one will die of hunger during those years of famine."

Pharaoh was convinced that Joseph's interpretation was the right one. That's because he could feel the presence of the Lord filling the room as Joseph was speaking! And it was God's very presence that gave Pharaoh testimony that Joseph's words were true. Joseph's interpretation gave Pharaoh peace and he had no doubt in his mind that Joseph was an extraordinary man.

Pharaoh looked at his servants and said to them, "Do you think we can find someone upon whom the Spirit of God rests as it does over this man?"

Surely, they all nodded "no," for Pharaoh said to Joseph: "If God showed you all these things, Joseph, then I don't see how there can be anyone wiser and more discreet than you. YOU are the one we need to be the ruler over my house, and the people must do everything you say. The only one who will have more authority than you is me. That's it. It's settled. You will be the new ruler over all of Egypt."

Pharaoh took off his royal ring and placed it on Joseph's finger so that all of Egypt would know that he was going to be the new man in charge.

As Joseph was taken throughout all of Egypt on the king's chariot, it's likely that he couldn't stop thinking about God's greatness in his life. In one day, God took Joseph out of prison and exalted him to be the second greatest man in all of Egypt!

## Only GOD could do something SO WONDERFUL!

## What Lessons Does GOD Have for Us?

⭐ **LESSON: FAITHFUL IN THE LITTLE**

In Joseph's life, we find many characteristics that the Lord also wants to form in us. The Lord has a promise for us if we, like Joseph, are faithful in the "smallest" and most "insignificant" things in our lives. Read the following verse:

*"His lord said unto him, Well done, thou good and faithful servant: thou hast been faithful over a few things, I will make thee ruler over many things: enter thou into the joy of thy Lord." (Matthew 25:21)*

It didn't matter whether Joseph was working in a great palace or in a dark dungeon. His work was important to him because he knew that his work had to be done for God, who is always watching us. For that reason, Joseph was faithful even in the smallest of things. To him, no job was too small or unimportant. Everything was important, and no matter how insignificant or unimportant the job seemed, Joseph was faithful to do it, and to do it right.

*"Servants, obey in all things your masters ... not ... as men pleasers ... but ... fearing God: And whatsoever ye do, do it heartily, as to the Lord." (Colossians 3:22-23)*

Joseph did just that. He worked hard and was faithful to the Lord, and the day did come when the Lord exalted him.

⭐ **LESSON: ALL THINGS WORK FOR GOOD**

Even though Joseph didn't deserve to be sold as a slave or thrown into prison, the Lord worked out each and every problem for good in his life.

But why?

*"And we know that all things work together for good to them that LOVE GOD, to them who are the called according to His purpose." (Romans 8:28, emphasis added)*

Joseph loved God with all of his heart, and God knew it. Even though God sent Joseph through hard times, everything worked out for good. GOD's perfect purposes and plans were accomplished.

It is the same in our lives. If we love the Lord and long to do His will, no matter what happens to us, those things will always work out for good in our lives.

## LESSON: **GOD'S WORK WAS COMPLETE**

God didn't want Joseph to suffer more than was necessary. He was just waiting for the right moment to take him out of prison. When Joseph finally lost hope in himself and completely surrendered his life to God's mercies, God took him out of the dungeon and placed him among princes.

> "He raises the poor from the dust And lifts the beggar from the ash heap,
> To set them among princes And make them inherit the throne of glory."
> (I Samuel 2:8a, NKJV)

## LESSON: **RESTING IN GOD**

Pharaoh called for Joseph because he had heard that God had given him a very special gift—the gift of understanding and interpreting dreams.

By the answer that Joseph gave to Pharaoh, we can see that Joseph was trusting in God alone for the interpretation of Pharaoh's dreams. He said to Pharaoh, *"It is not in me: God shall give Pharaoh an answer of peace."*

Why do you think God had given Joseph such a special gift? Because Joseph had allowed God to do His perfect work in him. In return, God had given Joseph the supernatural wisdom to see and know things the way HE does. It is one of several blessings we receive when we enter into God's rest (see pp. 52–53 of Bible Stories and Lessons, Book One).

### Years of Plenty and Years of Want

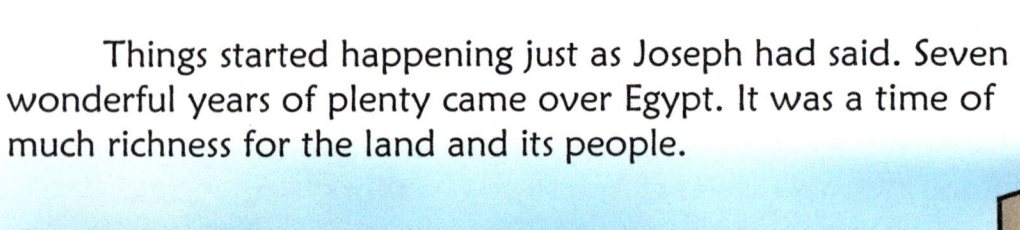

Things started happening just as Joseph had said. Seven wonderful years of plenty came over Egypt. It was a time of much richness for the land and its people.

Those were seven wonderful years in Joseph's life. Not only had the Lord taken him out of prison and made him the ruler over all of Egypt, but He also blessed him with a wife (Asenath) and gave him two sons. His firstborn son was named Manasseh, which means "causing to forget." Joseph gave him that name because it was during that time that God made Joseph forget all his toil (hard work) and all his father's house (his family).

32

Then Joseph named his second son Ephraim, which means "double fruit." Joseph named him that because God had made Joseph fruitful in the land of his affliction. That means that the Lord had **BLESSED** Joseph greatly in the same place where he had also **SUFFERED** greatly.

**Joseph was happy.** As always, he had done a wonderful job in storing away food for the years of famine that were soon to come. He had done SO well, in fact, that he and his men lost count as to how much they had gathered. There was so much food stored away that Egypt was more than ready for the years of hunger.

The years of plenty came to an end, and the time of famine started. There was no food to be found anywhere—except in Egypt. Because Joseph had stored up so much food, he was also able to sell grain to people who lived outside of Egypt. People from all around would go to Joseph to buy grain.

## Back in Canaan

It had been a long, long time since Joseph's brothers had sold him—about twenty years. Life went on in Canaan, however, and by then, most of Jacob's sons were married and had children of their own.

Even though Jacob was a very rich man, his money couldn't do much to help him during the famine because there just wasn't any food!

Things were getting rough for the family and Jacob was getting worried. He had heard that Egypt was selling food to people from surrounding countries, so he called for his sons and said to them: "What are you all doing just standing there and looking at each other for? We are all going to starve if we don't do something now! I have heard that there's grain in Egypt. I want all of you to go and see what you can buy. Benjamin will stay with me though. I don't want anything to happen to him."

Jacob's sons obeyed and headed for Egypt to see what they could find. Little did they know the great surprise that awaited them.

## Jacob's Sons Visit Egypt

As ruler over Egypt, Joseph was also in charge of deciding who he sold grain to. Every day he had to see lots and lots of people who came to him for food.

Joseph's brothers arrived safely in Egypt, and went straight to the line where people stood to request grain.

The day his brothers arrived, Joseph recognized them right away. Even though it had been a long time, they probably hadn't changed much. All ten of them stepped up and bowed down before him. They didn't recognize Joseph though, because he was dressed like an Egyptian and spoke in the Egyptian language. They could have never imagined that their brother was the governor over all the land of Egypt!

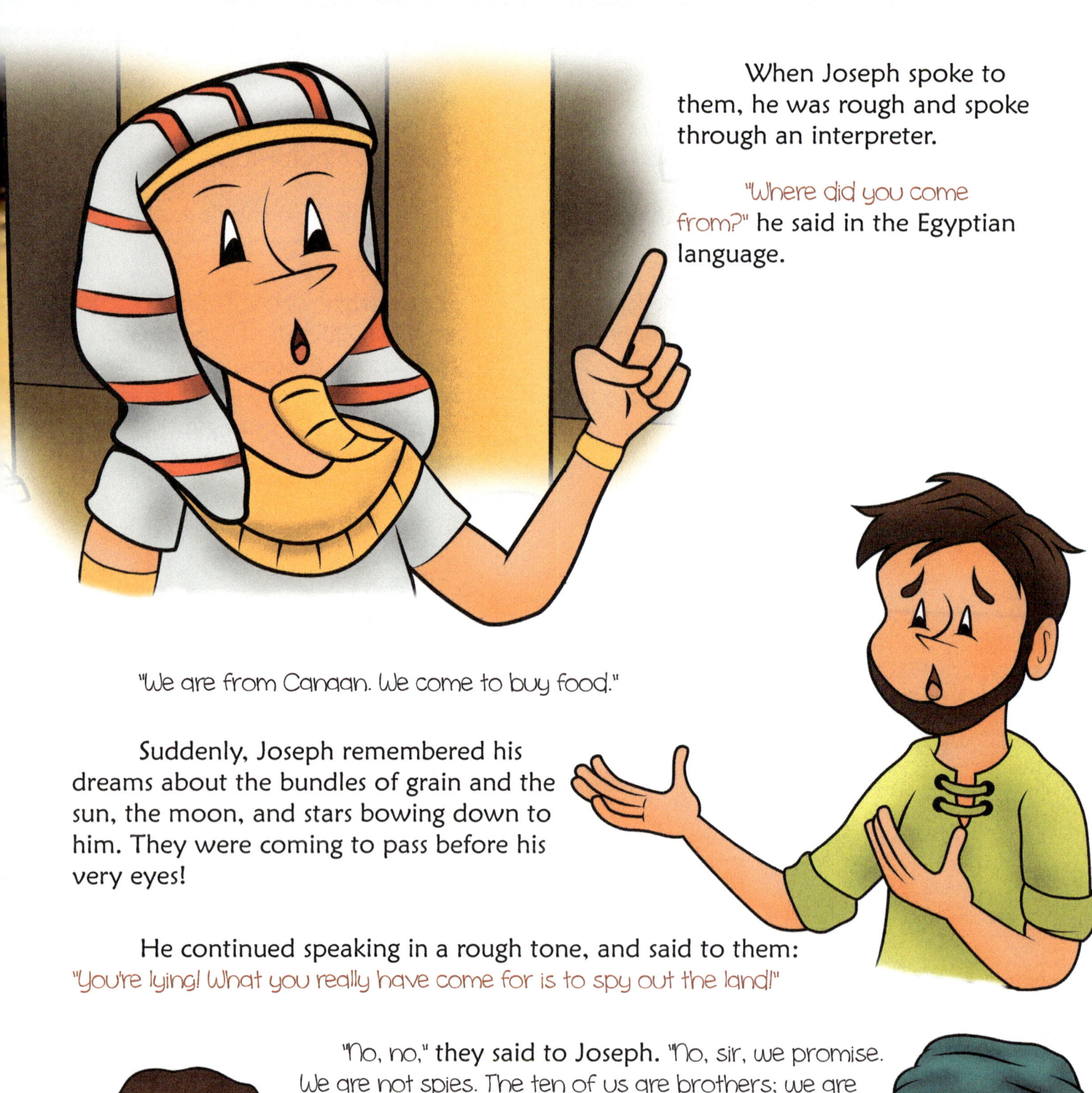

When Joseph spoke to them, he was rough and spoke through an interpreter.

"Where did you come from?" he said in the Egyptian language.

"We are from Canaan. We come to buy food."

Suddenly, Joseph remembered his dreams about the bundles of grain and the sun, the moon, and stars bowing down to him. They were coming to pass before his very eyes!

He continued speaking in a rough tone, and said to them:
"You're lying! What you really have come for is to spy out the land!"

"No, no," they said to Joseph. "No, sir, we promise. We are not spies. The ten of us are brothers; we are honest men, sir."

"No. I insist that you are spies," said Joseph.

"No, no. Please!" they said. "Let us explain. We are actually twelve brothers, but the youngest stayed home, and one is no longer with us."

Joseph said to them: "Well, we'll just have to see about that won't we? I still think you're spies so off to jail you go!"

Joseph put the brothers in jail for three days. On the third day, he called for them: "Listen, I fear God too, but I need to make sure you're telling me the truth. So, I'll tell you what—I'm going to let all of you, except for one, return home to bring your youngest brother back to me. I'll even give you grain to take back to your families, but if you don't bring your brother back here, you will never see my face again."

Joseph spoke to his brothers in the Egyptian language. An interpreter repeated Joseph's words in his brothers' language. His words were firm. That made the brothers worry! They began discussing the situation in front of Joseph. They had no idea that Joseph could understand everything they were saying!

"You see," said one, "this is happening to us because of what we did to Joseph. We saw the pain and the anguish he was going through, and we didn't listen to him when he cried out to us. That's why all of this is happening to us now!"

Then Reuben spoke up, "Didn't I tell you not to hurt him? You didn't listen to me though. And now, look at us. We're paying the price for his life!"

Joseph heard every word they said, and when he heard Reuben, it was too much for him. He stepped out of the room to find a place where he could cry.

When he finished crying, he went back to his brothers.

## WHO WOULD JOSEPH KEEP IN PRISON?

Since Reuben was the oldest brother, he was the one responsible for all of them, and, therefore, the one who should have been arrested. But Joseph probably didn't think it was fair since Reuben never wanted to hurt him in the first place. So instead, he had Simeon, the second oldest brother put in jail until they could bring Benjamin to Egypt.

Joseph's brothers couldn't believe what was happening. How would they explain all of this to Jacob, their father?

Joseph had the men's sacks filled with grain, and made sure one of his servants also put the money, with which they had paid for the grain, back into their bags. He also gave them food and water for their journey back home.

# What Lessons Does GOD Have for Us?

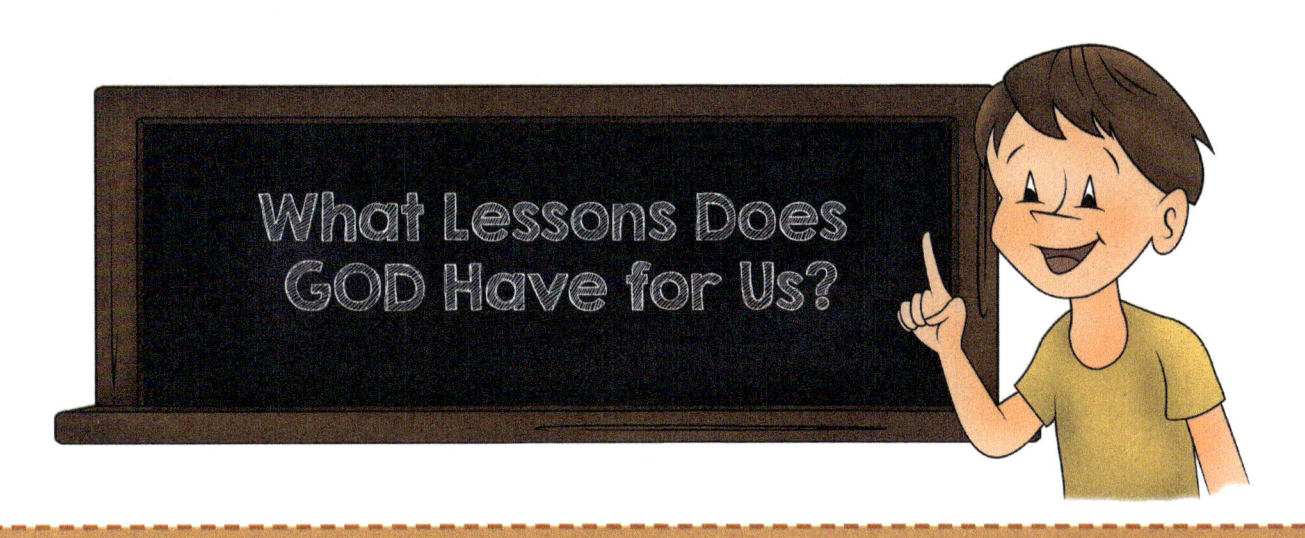

⭐ LESSON: **JOSEPH PUTS HIS BROTHERS TO THE TEST**

Joseph was rough with his brothers. He didn't reveal himself to them because he wanted to see if they had changed at all. He wanted to know if they were still the same hateful and envious men that he had known so many years before.

Joseph did several things to see what was in his brothers' hearts. First, he put them in jail for three days to see how they would react. Then, he put Simeon in jail and would not let him out unless the brothers returned with Benjamin. THEN he put all the brothers' money back into their sacks. He wanted to see if they were still those greedy, selfish men that loved money more than their brother.

## The Famine Worsens

After Joseph's brothers got back to Canaan, they told Jacob **EVERYTHING** that had happened. Jacob was devastated. He said: "First Joseph, now Simeon! And you still expect me to give you Benjamin so I can lose him also? Never. I will not let Benjamin go! I will die if something happens to him."

Reuben promised his father to bring Benjamin back safely, but Jacob refused to let him go.

Time passed and the food that Joseph had given them was running out. Jacob called for his sons and told them to go and buy food in Egypt again.

"But, father," they said to him, "the man in charge specifically told us NOT to return unless we came with our youngest brother."

Jacob was very sad about that, but he knew that if he didn't let Benjamin go, their family would starve. Judah felt terrible about all the hurt and pain that he had caused his father in selling Joseph as a slave. Because of that, he said to Jacob: "Father, I will be responsible for Benjamin's life. Send him with me; that way we can get food for our little ones and for ourselves also. Otherwise we'll all die here. But I promise you this, Father, if I don't bring Benjamin back to you, I will be the one to blame forever."

## Jacob had no choice but to let Benjamin go.

The brothers prepared gifts, honey, and spices to take to Egypt's ruler and twice as much money as they had taken the first time because they wanted to return the money they had found in their sacks.

## Jacob blessed his sons and said his good-byes.

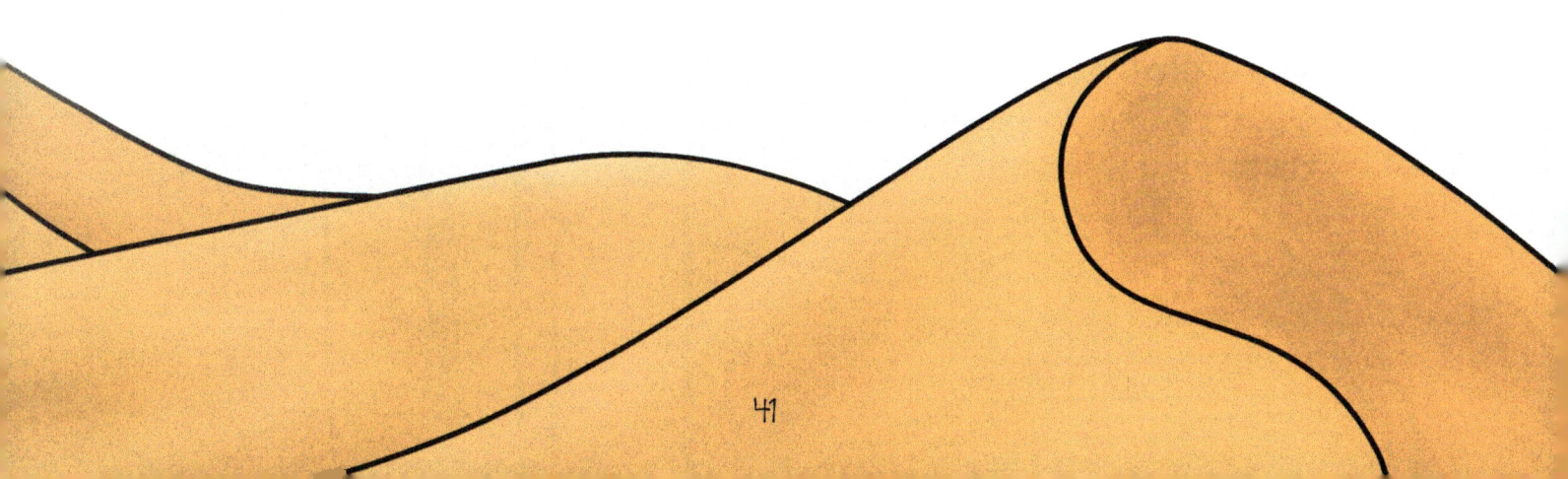

## Joseph and Benjamin Meet Again

Back in Egypt, Joseph probably started thinking that his brothers would never return for Simeon. After all, if they had been evil enough to sell him as a slave, it wouldn't be a problem for them to leave another brother as a prisoner.

But Joseph had most likely prayed to the Lord—asking that God **WOULD** cause them to return. He was anxious to see Benjamin and to know of his father's well-being. It had been SO long, and Joseph had been through SO much. There must have been moments in Joseph's life when he really wished he could laugh with his father and little brother again and share how he felt with them. Oh, he had missed them so!

On the day his brothers arrived, maybe Joseph even sat daydreaming—wondering when and if he would be so blessed as to see them again.

Suddenly, Joseph saw Benjamin and his brothers coming. His heart was full of memories and emotions! The moment he was waiting for had come.

Joseph quickly called his servant and said to him, "Make some meat and prepare a banquet; these men will have lunch with me today." The servant obeyed and took Joseph's brothers to his house.

It was a nerve-wracking moment for Jacob's sons. They were afraid because they thought, "He has brought us here because of the money that was in our sacks. And now he's probably going to keep us all as prisoners and slaves!"

As they waited at the door of the house, they tried to explain what had happened to Joseph's steward.

"We found the money in our sacks, but we promise we don't know who put it there. Really!"

"Relax," said the steward. "Your God must have put that money in your sacks. I received your money the first time."

The steward brought Simeon out to see them, gave them water to wash their feet, and gave them food for their donkeys. Then, he took them inside to the dining room.

The brothers had heard that Joseph was on his way home for lunch so they quickly prepared the gifts they had brought him.

When they saw Joseph, all of them bowed down to him. Joseph was anxious. He couldn't wait to ask them about Jacob. He asked, "How is your father? Is he well? Is he ... still alive?

"Yes. Our father is well and healthy."

How happy their answer must have made Joseph's heart! But then Joseph saw his dear little brother—Benjamin! And it almost seemed like too much to handle for one moment.

"This must be your younger brother that you spoke of?" he said to his brothers. "May God be gracious to you..."

But Joseph almost choked as he said it; he just couldn't take it anymore! He ran to another room and cried bitterly. And after crying for a time, he washed his face. When he was able to control himself, he went out to see his brothers again.

"Let's eat!" he said to his servants.

The brothers were each told where they should sit, but they couldn't believe it! For some reason, they had been placed in the exact same order that they had been born, from the oldest (Reuben) to the youngest (Benjamin)!

The food was placed on the table, but Joseph had told his servants to give Benjamin five times more food than his brothers. Once again, he wanted to test his brothers and see if they would still get jealous of their younger brother.

To Joseph's surprise, they didn't. They ate, drank, and were happy together.

# What Lessons Does GOD Have for Us?

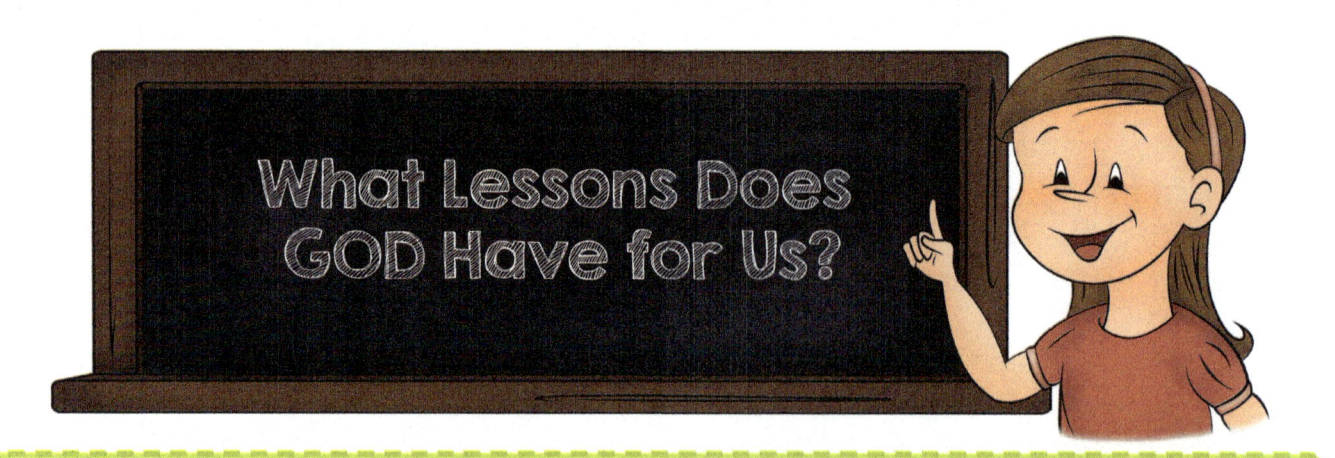

⭐ ## LESSON: THE BROTHERS REJOICE

When Joseph prepared a banquet for his brothers, he had his servants give five times more food to Benjamin than the others. Once again, Joseph was testing his brothers. He wanted to see if they were still the same envious and jealous men he had known as a young man.

To his surprise, God had done a wonderful work in them. Instead of getting angry, the brothers rejoiced when they saw the extra blessing that Benjamin received.

When we see our brothers and sisters in the Lord receiving a greater blessing than what we have received, the Lord is waiting for us to rejoice instead of being envious of them.

## Joseph's Silver Cup

Joseph had a plan up his sleeve. He wanted to be convinced that his brothers had changed, so he tested them one more time. He spoke to one of his servants in secret and said to him, "Go and fill the men's sacks with as much food as can fit. Then, take the money they gave you for the food and put it back in their sacks. Also, get my silver cup and put it in the youngest brother's sack."

The servant obeyed and did JUST as Joseph commanded.

Early the next morning, the brothers were on their way home. But just as they were leaving the city, Joseph told his steward to go and stop them. When the steward caught up with them, he said, "Why have you been so evil in stealing my master's cup? He was so kind to you!"

"Oh no, we wouldn't do such a thing!" they said. "We even brought the money back from the first time we found it in our sacks. We wouldn't steal from your master! In fact, feel free to search our bags. If you find the stolen item in one of our bags, not only should that man be put to death, but we will also become your servants."

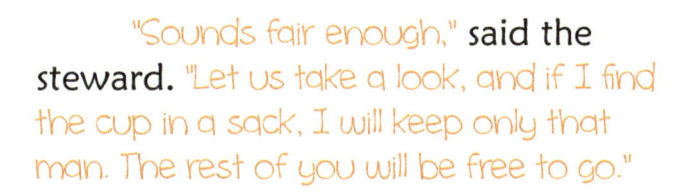

"Sounds fair enough," said the steward. "Let us take a look, and if I find the cup in a sack, I will keep only that man. The rest of you will be free to go."

The men hurried to put their sacks on the ground. Joseph's servant started with the oldest brother's sack and went one by one until he got to Benjamin's. When the brothers saw that the cup was in Benjamin's sack, they cried and tore their clothes as a sign of grief.

"NO! This can't be!" they cried out. "We can't let them take Benjamin. Let's go back to the city with him."

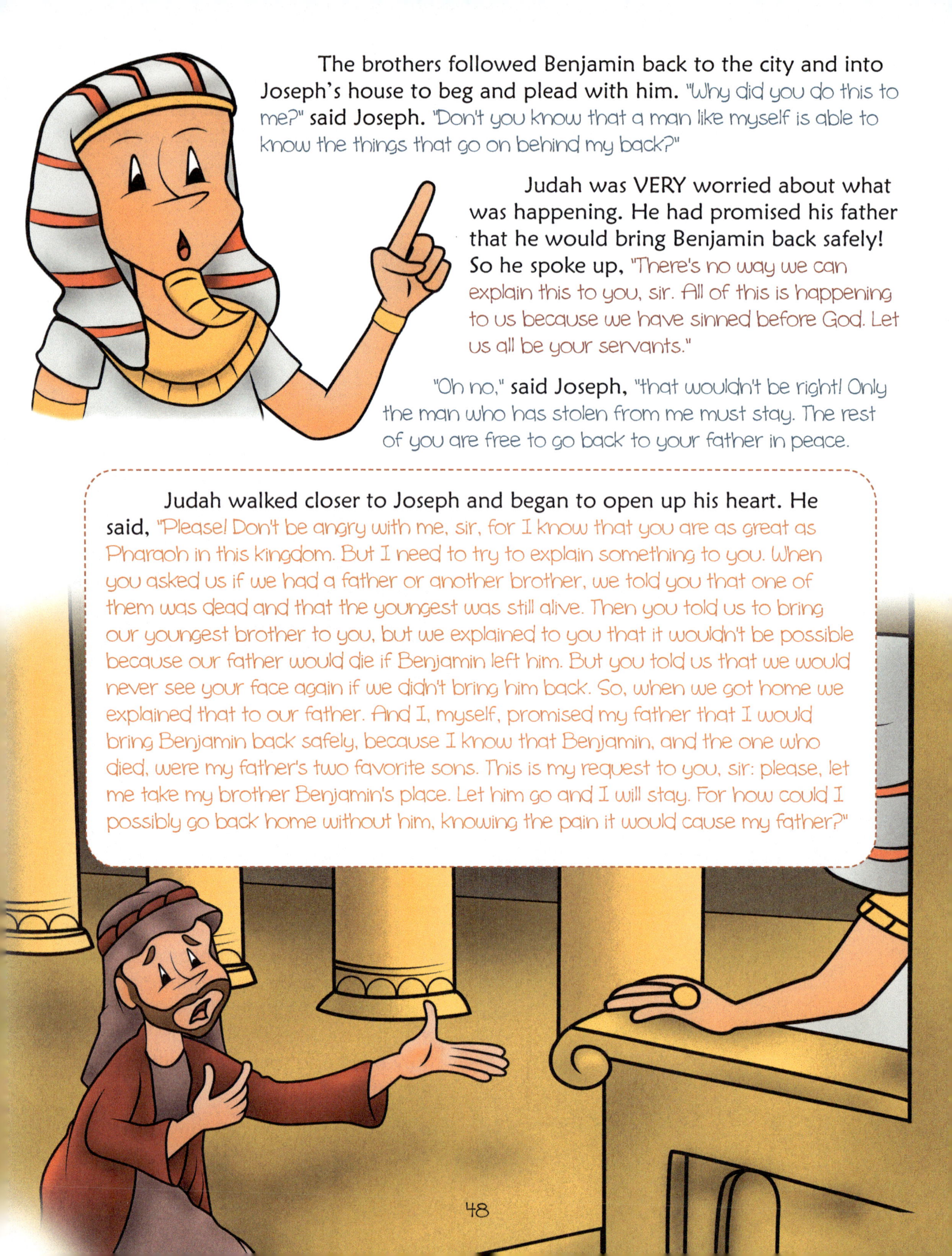

The brothers followed Benjamin back to the city and into Joseph's house to beg and plead with him. "Why did you do this to me?" said Joseph. "Don't you know that a man like myself is able to know the things that go on behind my back?"

Judah was VERY worried about what was happening. He had promised his father that he would bring Benjamin back safely! So he spoke up, "There's no way we can explain this to you, sir. All of this is happening to us because we have sinned before God. Let us all be your servants."

"Oh no," said Joseph, "that wouldn't be right! Only the man who has stolen from me must stay. The rest of you are free to go back to your father in peace."

Judah walked closer to Joseph and began to open up his heart. He said, "Please! Don't be angry with me, sir, for I know that you are as great as Pharaoh in this kingdom. But I need to try to explain something to you. When you asked us if we had a father or another brother, we told you that one of them was dead and that the youngest was still alive. Then you told us to bring our youngest brother to you, but we explained to you that it wouldn't be possible because our father would die if Benjamin left him. But you told us that we would never see your face again if we didn't bring him back. So, when we got home we explained that to our father. And I, myself, promised my father that I would bring Benjamin back safely, because I know that Benjamin, and the one who died, were my father's two favorite sons. This is my request to you, sir: please, let me take my brother Benjamin's place. Let him go and I will stay. For how could I possibly go back home without him, knowing the pain it would cause my father?"

Joseph's heart melted. He couldn't help himself anymore. Joseph asked everyone except his brothers to leave the room. Then, he began to cry and cry. He cried so loudly that everyone in the house could hear him!

Joseph's brothers probably looked at each other wondering what was going on. Suddenly Joseph looked at them and said, "I am Joseph. Is my father well?"

When the brothers realized that this ruler standing before them was their brother Joseph—the one they had sold so many years ago—they were speechless and terrified.

But Joseph wasn't angry with his brothers. He said to them, "Come closer brothers. I am your brother Joseph whom you sold to the merchants going to Egypt. But I don't want you to be sad or angry at yourselves for that, because..."

"God sent me before you to preserve a posterity for you in the earth, and to save your lives by a great deliverance. So now it was not you who sent me here, but God." (Genesis 45:7-8a, NKJV)

Joseph knew that God had allowed everything to take place as part of His perfect plan to save his whole family from hunger in the years of famine. He forgave his brothers because God had given him the grace to forget everything that had happened. Instead of blaming his brothers, he recognized that it had been God at work in his own life.

It was an incredible moment for all of them. Joseph hugged Benjamin and wept, and then he hugged his brothers and wept.

The news spread all the way to Pharaoh's house. Everyone was **HAPPY** that **JOSEPH** had been **REUNITED WITH HIS BROTHERS.**

# What Lessons Does GOD Have for Us?

## LESSON: THE SILVER CUP

Why do you think Joseph had his silver cup placed in Benjamin's sack?

Because he wanted to see how the other brothers would react when Benjamin was arrested. If they were still the same evil brothers from before, they would have been happy to get rid of another brother. That way, when they got back to Canaan, there would be even more inheritance for each of them.

What a surprise for Joseph to see how each and every one of them reacted. As soon as they saw the silver cup in Benjamin's sack, they tore their clothes!

In the Bible, when a person tore or ripped a piece of their clothing, it was an act showing that they felt much sadness or grief. Often people did it when someone had died or if they wanted to repent of their sins. It is like the saying we hear today, Joseph's brothers were "torn to pieces" when they saw what had happened.

Turns out they were NOT the same evil men they had once been. The hard trials that God had sent each one of them during those twenty something years had done a great work in their own lives.

## LESSON: JUDAH'S HEART WAS CHANGED

Judah knew how much his father would suffer if Benjamin was left in Egypt. He was truly worried about his father's well-being, so he pleaded with Joseph to let him stay as a slave in Egypt in place of Benjamin.

Judah's answer moved Joseph to tears, because Joseph could see that Judah was a changed man. Judah went from being a man full of hate and envy to a man full of love and unselfishness for his brothers.

God says that in order to fulfill all His law and commandments, we must do one thing: Love our neighbor as ourselves (Galatians 5:14).

Do you know what true love does? Read I Corinthians 13:4-7 (NKJV).

"Love suffers long and is kind; love does not envy; love does not parade itself, is not puffed up; does not behave rudely, does not seek its own, is not provoked, thinks no evil; does not rejoice in iniquity, but rejoices in the truth; bears all things, believes all things, hopes all things, endures all things."

The love of God is to always want the very best for our brothers and sisters in the Lord. The true love and maturity of God is just what Joseph found in his brothers' hearts.

## LESSON: FORGIVENESS

Earlier you heard that it displeases God when we hate our brother. What do you think God thinks when we don't want to forgive our brother?

"For if ye forgive men their trespasses, your heavenly Father will also forgive you: But if ye forgive not men their trespasses [offenses] neither will your Father forgive your trespasses." (Matthew 6:14-15)

Sometimes people do terrible things to us and offend us greatly. Few things could be as terrible as what Joseph's brothers did to him. Nonetheless, Joseph received a very special grace from the Lord to forgive and forget. Otherwise, he would not have named his first son Manasseh which means "causing to forget." It doesn't matter how terribly someone has hurt us; God can give us the same grace and power that he gave to Joseph to forgive and forget.

## Jacob and Joseph Together Again

Joseph's brothers probably felt great peace knowing that Joseph had forgiven them, and Joseph felt great joy in seeing his brothers again.

Joseph was still anxious about something though. He couldn't wait to see his father.

Even Pharaoh was happy for Joseph when he told him everything that had happened. Pharaoh said to him, "That's wonderful Joseph! You tell your brothers not to worry about a thing. Have them go and get your father. I will give them everything they need to bring your family back here. There's enough of everything for them here. I'll even give them a place to live."

Joseph told his brothers: "I want you to go and tell father that I am the ruler of Egypt. And tell him that I want all of you to come and live here in Egypt. You and your children can live in the land of Goshen. You will lack nothing here, for I will take care of you. Now go, take food for your trip and for your families and take wagons to bring them back here with you."

Joseph gave a brand new change of clothing to each one of his brothers, but to Benjamin he gave five changes of clothing and three hundred pieces of silver. He also sent lots of food and gifts to his father.

As the brothers reached Canaan, they must have felt **VERY NERVOUS.** How would they tell their father Jacob that they had lied to him all those years and that Joseph was still alive? What if he didn't believe them?

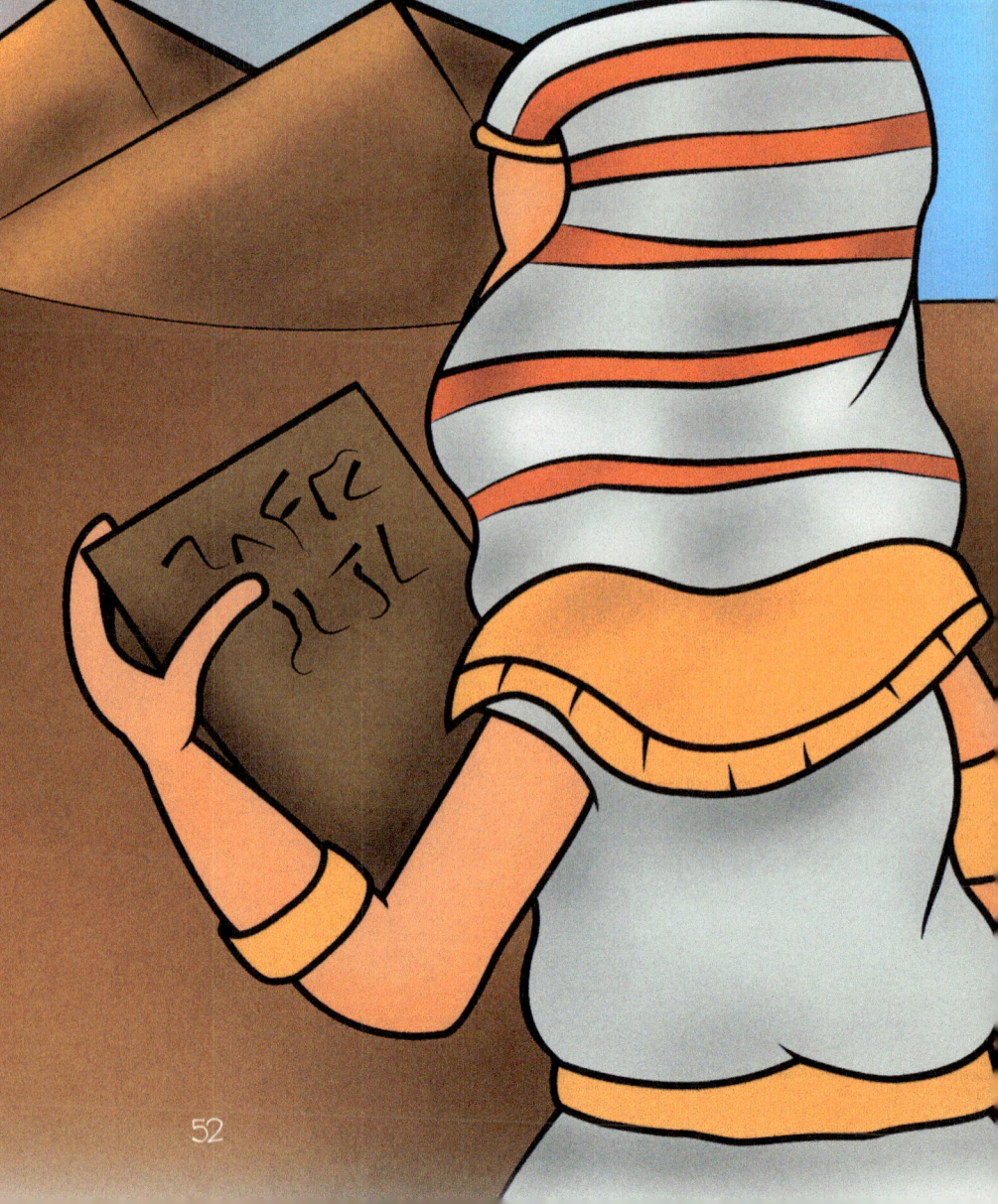

Jacob must have wondered why his sons were showing up with new clothes, so much delicious food to eat, so many donkeys, and Pharaoh's wagons.

"Father," they said to him, "we have something to tell you. It's that ... um ... um ... that ... well ... that, that, that ... well ... that Joseph is alive ... and ... um ... that he's ... um ... he's the ... he's the ... the ruler over all of Egypt."

# WHAT?

The news was too much for Jacob to hear. He truly could not believe it. But when he looked at the wagons that Pharaoh had sent, he thought: "It must be true. Otherwise, why would my sons be traveling in Pharaoh's wagons? My son is alive! My son is alive! Enough is enough! Let us all go to Egypt so I can see my son again before I die."

Jacob packed up his things and prepared his family for the big move to Egypt. They were sixty-six people in all!

During the trip, Jacob sought the Lord. He probably wanted to give God thanks and ask Him what he thought about all of this. And the Lord spoke to him that night through a dream. He told Jacob not to be afraid to go to Egypt. He promised Jacob that HE would go with him and that He would make Jacob a great nation there.

The big day when Joseph and Jacob would meet again finally arrived. What an exciting moment! Joseph hurried onto his chariot and went out to meet his family.

When he got off the chariot, he walked towards his father. He was probably already in tears. "Father. It is me-Joseph."

Jacob must have felt that he was living a dream! The two hugged. They were so happy to see each other that they just cried and cried and cried. What an unbelievable moment. The son Jacob had wept for throughout so many years was standing in front of him, and he had become one of the greatest men in all the land.

Pharaoh received Joseph's family with much kindness. He let them live in the best part of Egypt and Joseph made sure his family never lacked anything to eat.

## Jacob Dies

Jacob lived seventeen years in Egypt. God blessed him and his sons there in Egypt just as HE had promised. They grew to become a great and **MANY PEOPLE.**

One day, when Jacob was very old and lying on his death bed, Joseph went to visit him. He took his two sons, Manasseh and Ephraim, with him. Jacob couldn't see well anymore because of his old age, so he asked, "Who is this that you brought with you, Joseph?"

"My sons, Manasseh and Ephraim, father."

Then, Jacob said to Joseph: "Joseph, the Lord gave me a promise when I was in the city of Luz. He told me that He would bless me and my seed after me, and that he was going to give me the land of Canaan, the land that he promised to my fathers as a possession for me and for my children after me. Your two sons are as my sons, so that means that they, too, ought to receive part of that blessing. Bring them to me."

Jacob blessed Joseph and his sons saying: "The God of my grandfather Abraham and of my father Isaac has guided me all my life and has sent His Angel to protect me from all evil at all times. May that same God bless you two young boys. May my name and my fathers' names be remembered through you both, and may you have many children."

Then Jacob called for all of his sons and prophesied over each one of them. He blessed some of them, and he scolded some of them, but not one of them received a blessing as great as Joseph's blessing. After he finished giving the blessings to his sons, Jacob curled back into his bed and passed away. Although Jacob saw much hardship in his life, the Lord gave him peace and blessings in his last years. Joseph buried Jacob in the same cave where Abraham was buried.

## Joseph's Last Days

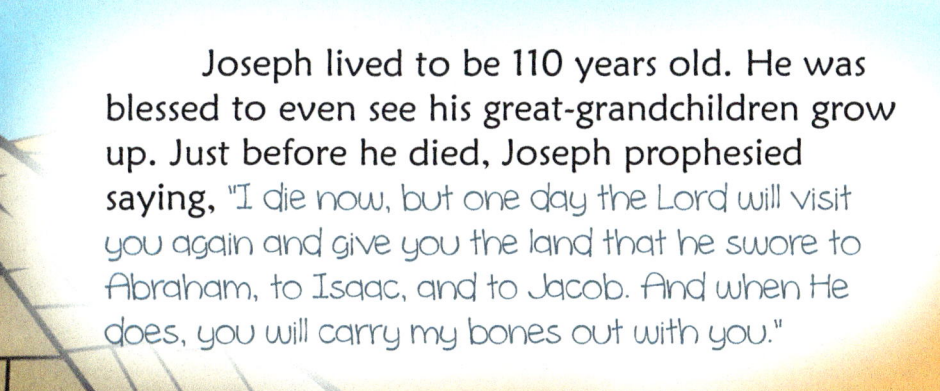

Joseph lived to be 110 years old. He was blessed to even see his great-grandchildren grow up. Just before he died, Joseph prophesied saying, "I die now, but one day the Lord will visit you again and give you the land that he swore to Abraham, to Isaac, and to Jacob. And when He does, you will carry my bones out with you."

Years later the people of Israel would see that prophecy come to pass just as Joseph said.

Much like Jesus, Joseph went through much suffering and pain in his life. But even though it hurt him greatly to be separated from his family, God also allowed it for a **VERY GREAT PURPOSE**—to one day save his family's life.

And even though Joseph felt all alone at times, the Lord was ALWAYS by his side, and his broken and humble heart became something irresistible to God. In the end, Joseph not only became a very great ruler, but he also became a very great man in God's eyes.

"...a broken and a contrite heart, O God, thou wilt not despise."
(Psalm 51:17)

# What Lessons Does GOD Have for Us?

## LESSON: JOSEPH IS A FIGURE OF CHRIST

Remember that in the story of the creation, we studied that Joseph was the seventh man of faith? He represents the perfect man that has entered into God's rest, is dead to his own works, and is alive to God and others. That means that Joseph had gone through the seven steps of creation in his spiritual life and God's life had been formed in him. Like Christ, Joseph shows us the journey, or the way, to reaching spiritual perfection and the authority of God's kingdom.

Read the following list to see how Joseph and Jesus lived through the same experiences.

1. Joseph and Jesus were both greatly loved by their fathers. (Genesis 37:3; Matthew 3:17)
2. Both of them were sent to seek out their brothers. (Genesis 37:13-17; John 1:11)
3. Both of them were hated by their brothers who wanted to kill them. (Genesis 37:18; John 8:40, 59)
4. Both of them had brothers who were rebellious against God's plan. (Genesis 37:20; Matthew 28:11-15)
5. Both had their coats taken away. (Genesis 37:23; Matthew 27:35)
6. Both were thrown into a deep pit. (Genesis 37:24; Jonah 2:6; Matthew 12:40)
7. Both were sold for silver. (Genesis 37:28; Matthew 26:14-15)
8. Both were separated from their fathers. (Genesis 37:28-36; Mark 15:33-34)
9. Both were falsely accused. (Genesis 39:11-20; Matthew 26:59-60)
10. Both were taken to Egypt. (Genesis 37:28; Revelation 11:8)
11. Both forgave their brothers. (Genesis 45:5, 50:16-21; Luke 23:34)
12. Both received the authority of the kingdom. (Genesis 41:41; Matthew 28:18; I Peter 3:22)
13. Just as every Egyptian bowed down before Joseph, so every knee shall bow down before the Lord Jesus Christ. (Genesis 41:43; Philippians 2:10)
14. Both received a new name. (Genesis 41:45; Philippians 2:9)

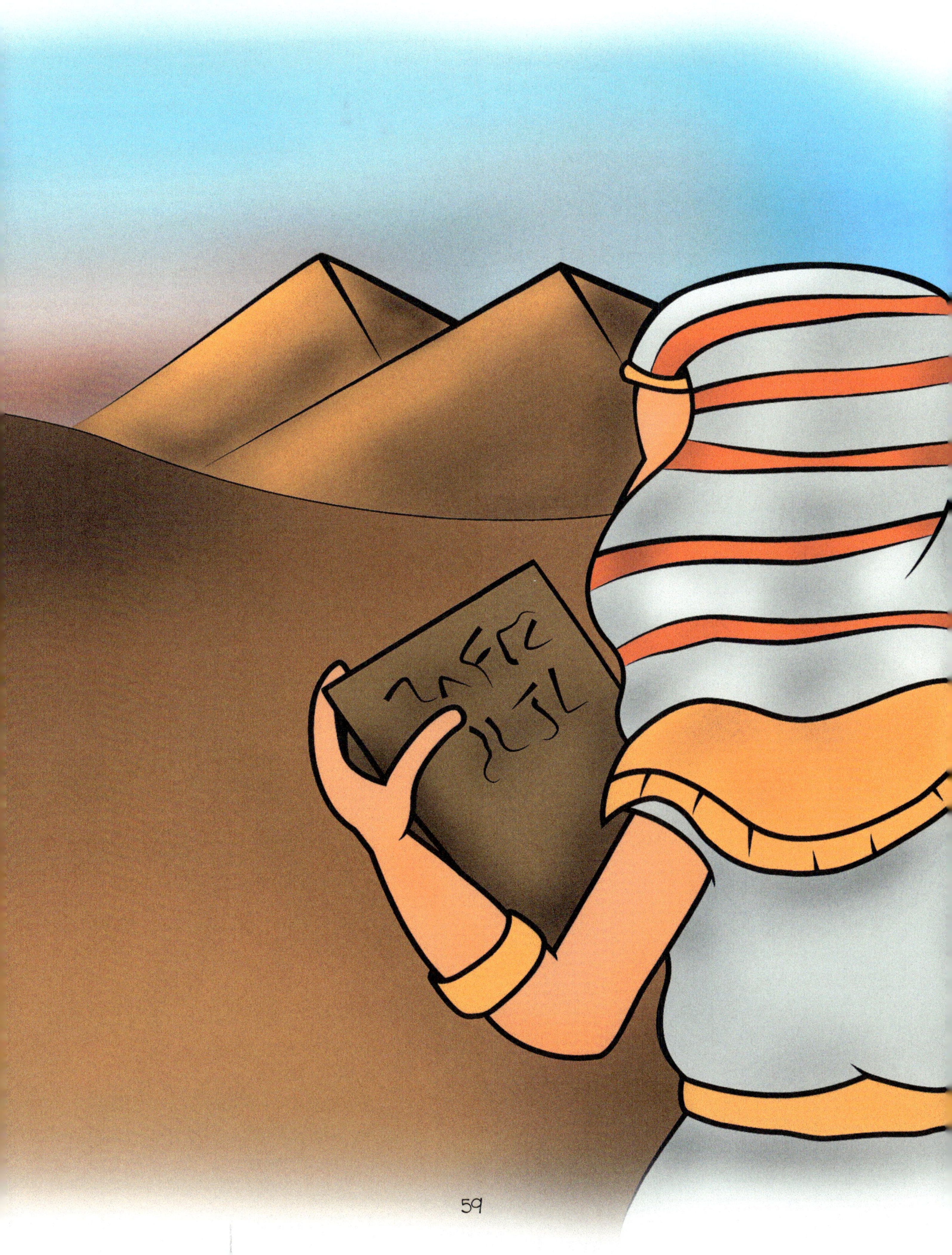

**Bible Stories and Lessons**

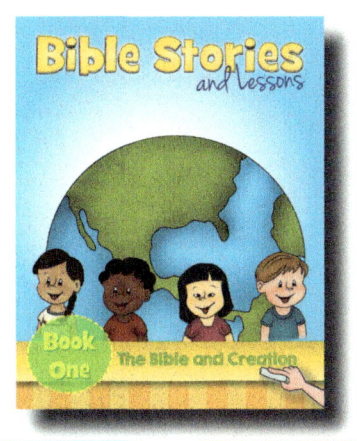

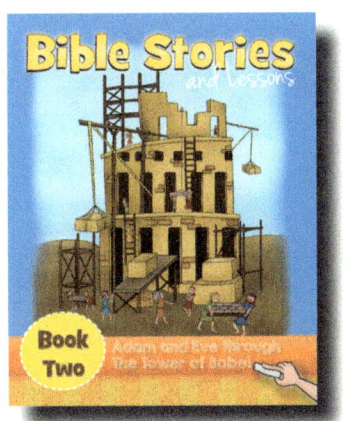

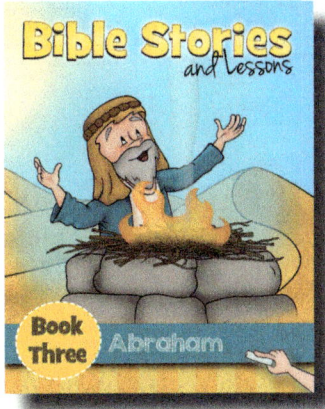

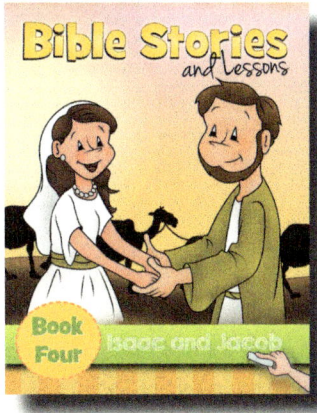

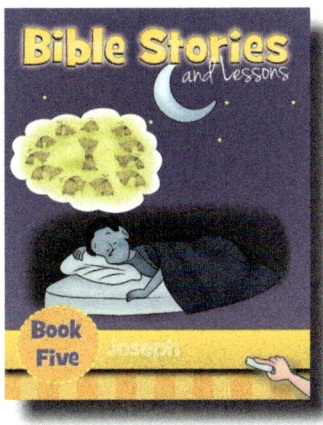

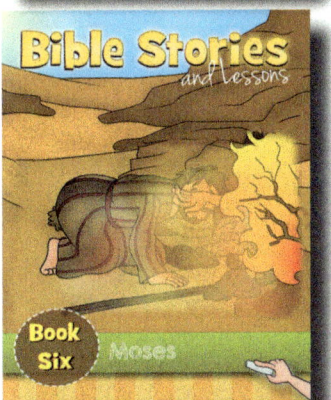

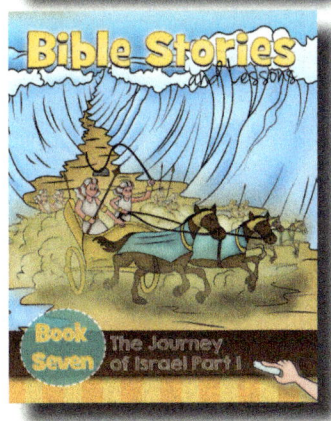

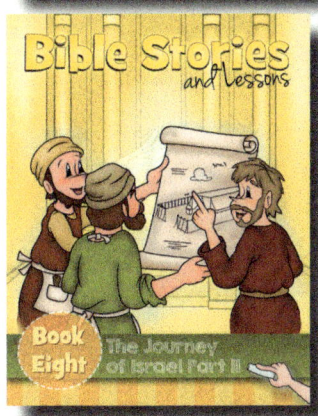

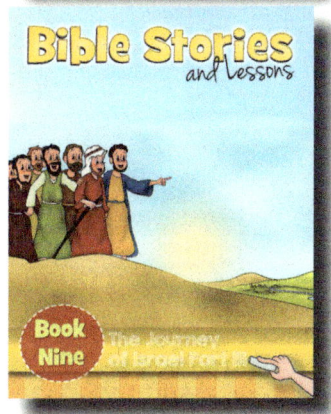

- Book One: The Bible and Creation
- Book Two: Adam and Eve Through The Tower of Babel
- Book Three: Abraham
- Book Four: Isaac and Jacob
- Book Five: Joseph
- Book Six: Moses
- Book Seven: The Journey of Israel Part I
- Book Eight: The Journey of Israel Part II
- Book Nine: The Journey of Israel Part III

*Download FREE Interactive Guide!*

**Available in English and Spanish at:**

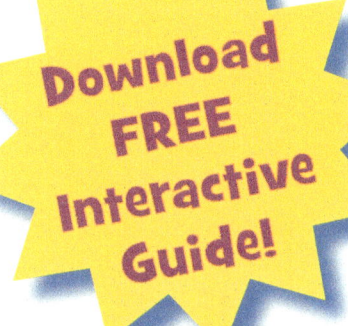

# HEBRON MINISTRIES
"...Christ in you, the hope of glory." Colossians 1:27

**Halo Publishing International**
www.halopublishing.com

eBooks at: **nook** by Barnes & Noble  **amazon** kindle

https://store.hebronministries.com/books.html
1-800-527-8329

CPSIA information can be obtained at www.ICGtesting.com
Printed in the USA
LVOW05s2125240915

455555LV00007B/9/P